Questions AND Answers

OCEANS AND RIVERS

Barbara Taylor

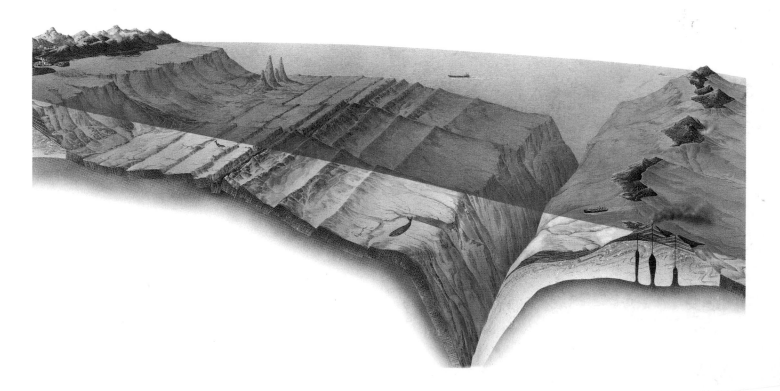

KINGFISHER

NEW YORK

KINGFISHER
a Houghton Mifflin Company imprint
215 Park Avenue South
New York, New York 10003
www.houghtonmifflinbooks.com

First published in 2002
10 9 8 7 6 5 4 3 2 1

1TR/0402/TIMS/UNI/130MA

LIBRARY OF CONGRESS CATALOGING-IN-PUBLICATION DATA
has been applied for.

ISBN 0-7534-5491-2

Printed in China

Author: Barbara Taylor
Editors: John Birdsall, Jennie Morris, and Hannah Wilson
Coordinating Editor: Sarah Snavely
Designer: Joe Conneally
DTP Coordinator: Sarah Pfitzner
Artwork Archivists: Wendy Allison and Steve Robinson
Production Controller: Jo Blackmore

The publishers wish to thank Philip L. Woodworth at
Proudman Oceanographic Laboratory, Birkenhead, England

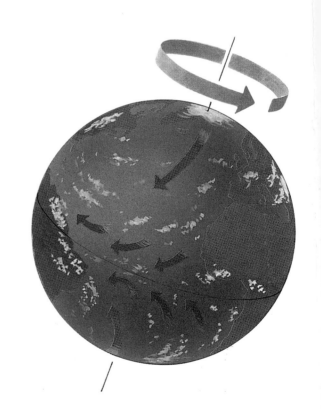

Contents

Water in Our World

Three quarters of Earth's surface is covered by water—and nearly all of it is contained in the oceans and seas. The rest, a very small amount, is in the air or froze long ago to form the polar ice caps. Most of the water we use comes from rivers and lakes or has seeped through rocks and collected underground.

How do people use rivers?

Rivers are used for a wide range of purposes—they provide water for drinking, washing, and watering crops, and large rivers are often used as highways. Transportation vessels carry people and cargo from place to place. Some fast-flowing rivers are harnessed to generate electricity, while others offer recreational activities such as canoeing, swimming, and rafting.

How much of the world's water is salty?

About 97 percent of all water is the salty water of the oceans and seas. The sea is salty because salts are either washed off of the land by rivers or escape from cracks in the ocean floor. Other salts come from undersea volcanoes.

Salty seawater (97%)

Freshwater as ice (2%)

Fresh liquid water (1%)

What is the water cycle?

The movement of water between the land, the sea, and the air is called the water cycle (right). As the Sun heats the water in oceans, rivers, lakes, and plants, some of the water evaporates, changing into water vapor (a gas) and rising into the air. High up in the sky the water vapor cools and changes back into tiny drops of liquid water. This process is called condensation. The water drops join to make clouds and eventually fall as rain, hail, or snow. The cycle then starts all over again. As a result of this recycling, the amount of water on Earth always remains the same.

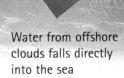

Water evaporates from plants

Water evaporates from oceans and seas

Water from offshore clouds falls directly into the sea

Do all living things need water?

Water makes up the greatest part of the bodies of plants and animals and is vital for all life. Did you know that your body is made up of more than 70 percent water? You need to drink about 0.5 gallons (2L) of water a day and much more when it is hot or you are working hard. Aquatic animals live surrounded by water, but those that live on land have to find water (right) or get all that they need from their food.

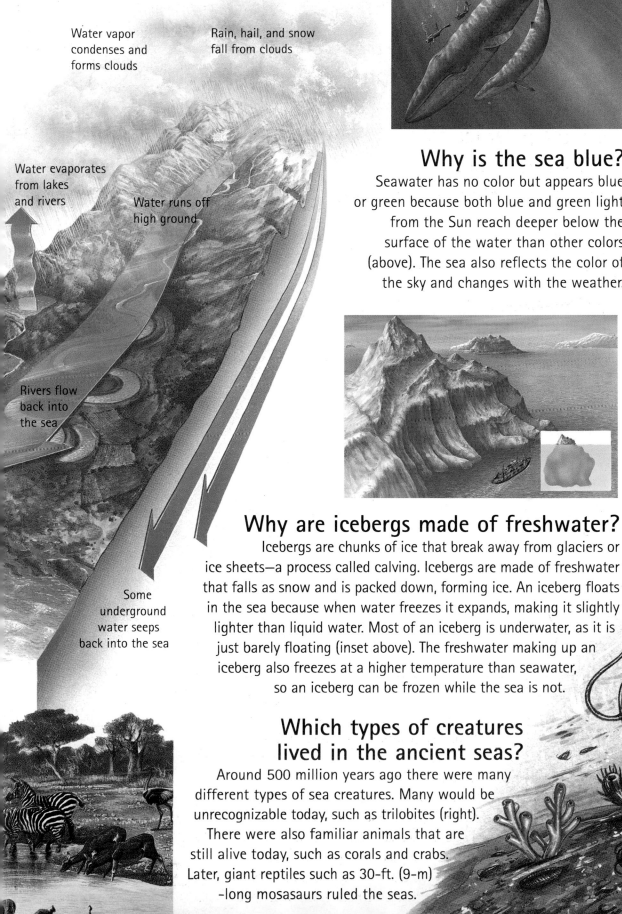

Water vapor condenses and forms clouds

Rain, hail, and snow fall from clouds

Water evaporates from lakes and rivers

Water runs off high ground

Rivers flow back into the sea

Some underground water seeps back into the sea

Why is the sea blue?

Seawater has no color but appears blue or green because both blue and green light from the Sun reach deeper below the surface of the water than other colors (above). The sea also reflects the color of the sky and changes with the weather.

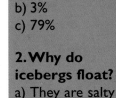

Quick-fire Quiz

1. How much of the world's water is fresh?
a) 5%
b) 3%
c) 79%

2. Why do icebergs float?
a) They are salty
b) They are lighter than water
c) Water is heavier when frozen

3. Which of these animals lived in the seas long ago?
a) Trilobites
b) Hexabites
c) Quadubites

4. What is water in gas form called?
a) Sparkling water
b) Water vapor
c) Condensation

Why are icebergs made of freshwater?

Icebergs are chunks of ice that break away from glaciers or ice sheets—a process called calving. Icebergs are made of freshwater that falls as snow and is packed down, forming ice. An iceberg floats in the sea because when water freezes it expands, making it slightly lighter than liquid water. Most of an iceberg is underwater, as it is just barely floating (inset above). The freshwater making up an iceberg also freezes at a higher temperature than seawater, so an iceberg can be frozen while the sea is not.

Which types of creatures lived in the ancient seas?

Around 500 million years ago there were many different types of sea creatures. Many would be unrecognizable today, such as trilobites (right). There were also familiar animals that are still alive today, such as corals and crabs. Later, giant reptiles such as 30-ft. (9-m) -long mosasaurs ruled the seas.

5

World's Oceans

With more than 70 percent of its surface covered by water, planet Earth could be renamed planet Ocean. The relationship between water and the land has, however, been an ever changing one. Over millions of years sea levels have risen and fallen as the climate has changed, and the pattern of land and water has altered as continents have slowly drifted apart on their own oceans of molten rock.

The Arctic Ocean is the world's smallest and shallowest ocean. It holds only one percent of Earth's seawater—still 25 times more water than is found in all of the world's rivers and lakes! The Arctic Ocean is covered by thick ice for six months of the year (right). This ice covers an area one-and-a-half times the size of Canada.

Is the Atlantic getting wider?

The North Atlantic Ocean, which separates Europe and Africa from North America, is growing wider by around 1.2 in. (3cm) a year. This is because the continents of Europe and Africa are drifting away from North America, causing the ocean floor to crack open in the middle. Molten rock has flowed into this crack (right), producing new ocean floor, while the crust on each side of the new floor has been lifted up into a huge mountain range called the Mid-Atlantic Ridge. These mountains stretch for more than 6,800 mi. (11,000km), and some of the peaks stand 2.5 mi. (4km) tall.

When part of the ocean floor slides beneath a continent, a deep trench may form.

How have the world's oceans changed?

Over millions of years heat from inside Earth has made the continents drift around the surface of the globe, changing the size and shape of the oceans. About 420 million years ago the oceans surrounded four separate land masses. But by 200 million years ago these land masses had drifted together, and a single vast ocean lapped the shores of a new supercontinent called Pangaea. Over the next 150 million years Pangaea began to break up, giving us the pattern of land and sea that we have today.

Pangaea

Molten rock rises up to fill in the crack in the ocean floor.

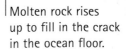

Which is the largest ocean?

The Pacific is the world's largest ocean, covering about one third of Earth. It is bigger than all of the continents put together. The Pacific is also the deepest ocean, with an average depth of 14,040 ft. (4,280m), but descending to 36,160 ft. (11,022m) in the Mariana Trench off the coast of the Philippines—the deepest of all the ocean trenches. The Pacific is dotted with thousands of islands, including the Hawaiian and the Galapagos Islands. It also contains the world's largest coral reef—the Great Barrier Reef.

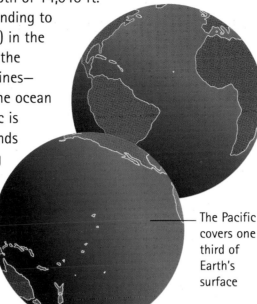

The Pacific covers one third of Earth's surface

Where two parts of the ocean floor move apart, a crack forms into which hot, molten rock swells up to make a ridge.

How do seas differ from oceans?

Seas are smaller areas of saltwater usually close to, or surrounded by, land. There are about 70 seas altogether. Some, such as the Caspian Sea, are totally surrounded by land. Others, such as the North Sea, are only partly enclosed by land. The South China Sea, at nearly 1.16 million sq. mi. (3 million sq km), is the largest sea on Earth, yet it is only one fifth the size of the smallest ocean.

How many oceans are there?

Some geographers say that our planet has only three true oceans—the Pacific Ocean, which contains more than half of the seawater on Earth, the Atlantic Ocean, and the Indian Ocean. They believe that the other so-called oceans are simply part of the "big three." Most maps, however, not only split the Atlantic into two—the North Atlantic Ocean and the South Atlantic Ocean—but also include two much smaller oceans, the Arctic Ocean and the Antarctic (or Southern) Ocean (right).

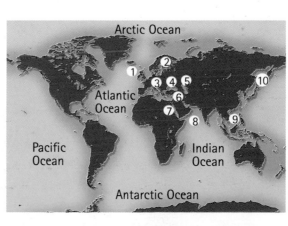

Arctic Ocean
Atlantic Ocean
Pacific Ocean
Indian Ocean
Antarctic Ocean

Quick-fire Quiz

1. Which is the largest sea in the world?
a) The North Sea
b) The South China Sea
c) The Dead Sea

2. How much of Earth's seawater is in the Arctic Ocean?
a) 1%
b) 10%
c) 25%

3. In which ocean is the Great Barrier Reef?
a) Atlantic Ocean
b) Pacific Ocean
c) Indian Ocean

4. How much wider is the Atlantic Ocean growing each year?
a) 12 in. (30cm)
b) 1.2 in. (3cm)
c) 120 in. (300cm)

MAP KEY
1. North Sea
2. Baltic Sea
3. Adriatic Sea
4. Black Sea
5. Caspian Sea
6. Dead Sea
7. Red Sea
8. Arabian Sea
9. South China Sea
10. Sea of Okhotsk

Seas of the World

Seas are usually smaller parts of oceans—often close to or partly surrounded by land. The North Sea, for example, is part of the Atlantic Ocean that lies between Britain and mainland Europe. Some seas, however, such as the Dead Sea and the Caspian Sea, are really just large saltwater lakes.

How many seas are there?

Ancient sailors once talked about sailing the Seven Seas—the Red Sea, the Mediterranean Sea, the Persian Gulf, the Black Sea, the China Sea, the Caspian Sea, and the Indian Ocean. These were the only seas that were widely known at that time. Today we know of many more seas than this, and although oceanographers disagree on the exact number, it is generally accepted that there are about 70 in total.

How big is the Caspian Sea?

The Caspian Sea (above) is the largest inland sea on Earth, covering 163,013 sq. mi. (422,170 sq km). Its surface area is four times bigger than that of the largest lake—Lake Superior. Over the past five million years the Caspian Sea has sometimes been linked to the world's oceans through the Sea of Azov, the Black Sea, and the Mediterranean Sea. Today it is almost completely landlocked.

Why is the Red Sea so salty?

The Red Sea contains some of the saltiest seawater in the world. This is partly because volcanoes on the seafloor add salts to the water, and also because the Red Sea is in an area with a hot, dry climate. The Sun constantly evaporates freshwater from the surface of the Red Sea into the air—leaving the salts behind. Local people often use the Sun's power in this way to extract salt for themselves (left). By building shallow pools, the speed of evaporation can be increased, and the salt that is left behind can easily be raked up and collected.

What is so strange about the Sargasso Sea?

The Sargasso Sea is part of the Atlantic Ocean, between the West Indies and the Azores, where the water is very calm. Sailors used to dread this area, where they would often find themselves engulfed in thick mists, among rafts of rotting seaweed. But for the freshwater eels of North America and Europe (left), the Sargasso Sea holds a unique attraction—it is to here that they migrate to mate and spawn before dying. Only the young eels make the return trip of up to 7,460 mi. (12,000km)—miraculously managing to find their way back to the rivers from where their parents came.

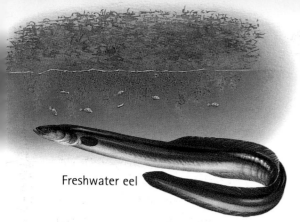

Freshwater eel

How has the Mediterranean Sea changed?

About six million years ago the Mediterranean Sea was cut off from the Atlantic Ocean by rising mountains. One thousand years later the water had all evaporated—leaving a dry seabed covered in salt. About a million years later the sea level rose in the Atlantic Ocean until it began to pour over the mountains—creating the greatest waterfall in Earth's history (right). It took about 100 years for the Mediterranean Sea to fill up completely.

Quick-fire Quiz

1. Which is the world's largest inland sea?
a) South China Sea
b) North Sea
c) Caspian Sea

2. When was the Mediterranean Sea cut off from the Atlantic?
a) 1 million years ago
b) 8 million years ago
c) 6 million years ago

3. How many more times saltier than typical seawater is the water of the Dead Sea?
a) 100 times
b) 25 times
c) 5 times

4. Which sea is the breeding place for freshwater eels?
a) Sargasso Sea
b) Dead Sea
c) Red Sea

How did the Dead Sea get its name?

The Dead Sea, between Israel and Jordan, got its name because its waters are so salty that nothing lives in it for very long. Its water is five times saltier than that of most other oceans. Rivers flowing into the Dead Sea bring with them salt from rocks high up in the mountains. The salt makes the water in the Dead Sea so heavy and dense that people swimming in it float easily (right).

The Ocean Floor

Hidden deep beneath the oceans lies a landscape far more dramatic than the one we see above the waves. Here the mountain ranges are larger, the valleys deeper, the slopes steeper, and the plains wider. With no wind, rain, or ice to wear away the rocks, this undersea world is rough-edged and slow to change. But it is not without its own powerful forces. Ocean currents scour the seabed and deposit huge amounts of sediments, while fiery underwater volcanoes spout rivers of molten rock, and hot springs bubble in the depths.

Why do deep-sea fish glow in the dark?

More than half of all deep-sea fish glow in the dark of the ocean depths. Some produce light by means of chemical reactions inside their bodies. Other fish have bacteria inside them that makes them glow—helping the fish to find food and a mate, or to scare off attackers in a world of perpetual night.

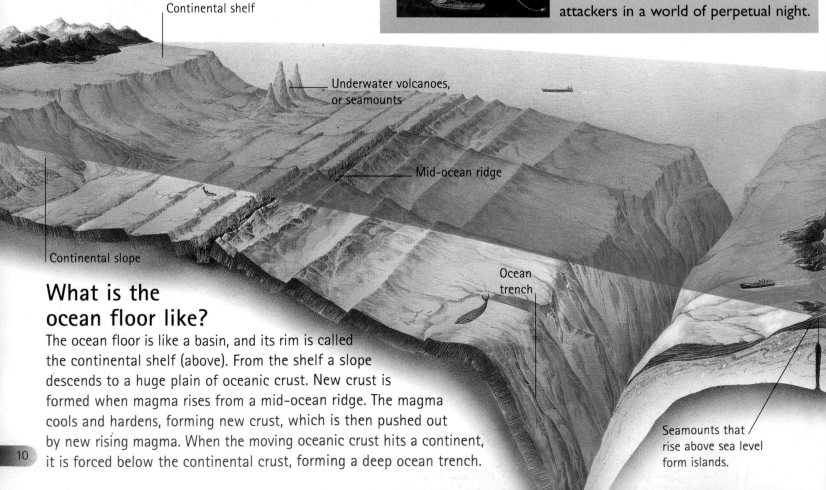

Continental shelf

Underwater volcanoes, or seamounts

Mid-ocean ridge

Continental slope

Ocean trench

Seamounts that rise above sea level form islands.

What is the ocean floor like?

The ocean floor is like a basin, and its rim is called the continental shelf (above). From the shelf a slope descends to a huge plain of oceanic crust. New crust is formed when magma rises from a mid-ocean ridge. The magma cools and hardens, forming new crust, which is then pushed out by new rising magma. When the moving oceanic crust hits a continent, it is forced below the continental crust, forming a deep ocean trench.

How do rivers create canyons under the sea?

Rivers wash huge amounts of sediments into the sea, where they build up on the continental shelf—the shallow ledge surrounding the land. If this sediment piles up too high or is disturbed by an earthquake, it may begin to move. This results in a turbidity current—a massive amount of water and sediment that slides across the continental shelf. Turbidity currents can travel at up to 55 mph (90km/h) and have huge erosive power, carving out narrow, steep-sided canyons in much the same way as rivers do on land.

A turbidity current carves out a canyon as it flows downhill.

Which is Earth's tallest mountain?

Even though Mount Everest is considered to be the tallest mountain on Earth, there is an underwater mountain that is even bigger. Mauna Kea, a gigantic volcano in the Pacific Ocean, rises an incredible 6.37 mi. (10.252km) above the seabed—over 0.6 mi. (1km) taller than Mount Everest! The 2.61 mi. (4.205km) of Mauna Kea that is above sea level forms the tropical island of Hawaii. Mauna Kea means White Mountain in Hawaiian because its peak is often snowcapped.

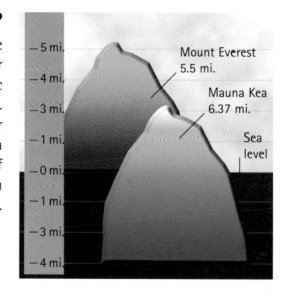

— 5 mi.
— 4 mi.
— 3 mi.
— 1 mi.
— 0 mi.
— 1 mi.
— 3 mi.
— 4 mi.

Mount Everest 5.5 mi.

Mauna Kea 6.37 mi.

Sea level

What are black smokers?

In the darkness of the ocean, some 10,000 ft. (3,000m) down, chimneys spew out what looks like black smoke. These chimneys form when boiling hot water gushes up through cracks called deep-sea vents in the seabed. The hot water spurting out of the top of the chimneys is black with mineral-rich particles. Some of these minerals are deposited around the vents, building up to form tall chimneys. Black smokers occur near mid-ocean ridges where two plates are pulling apart. Giant tube worms, clams, and other strange marine creatures live in the mineral-rich waters around black smokers.

Islands and Reefs

Islands form in many ways. Those near the shore may be chunks of land that have broken away from a continent or simply parts of the mainland cut off by rising sea levels. Ocean islands, far away from any land, are usually the tops of underwater volcanoes. Coral islands, called atolls, are the remains of reefs around submerged volcanoes.

How do coral atolls form?

1 Coral often grows on the shores of volcanic islands where the water is shallow, warm, and rich in minerals. Over hundreds or thousands of years the island may sink or the sea level may rise.

2 The coral grows together with tiny plants called algae, which need sunshine to develop. The reef constantly grows up toward the Sun.

3 When the island finally disappears beneath the waves, a deep ring of coral— or an atoll—which surrounds a shallow central lagoon, is left behind.

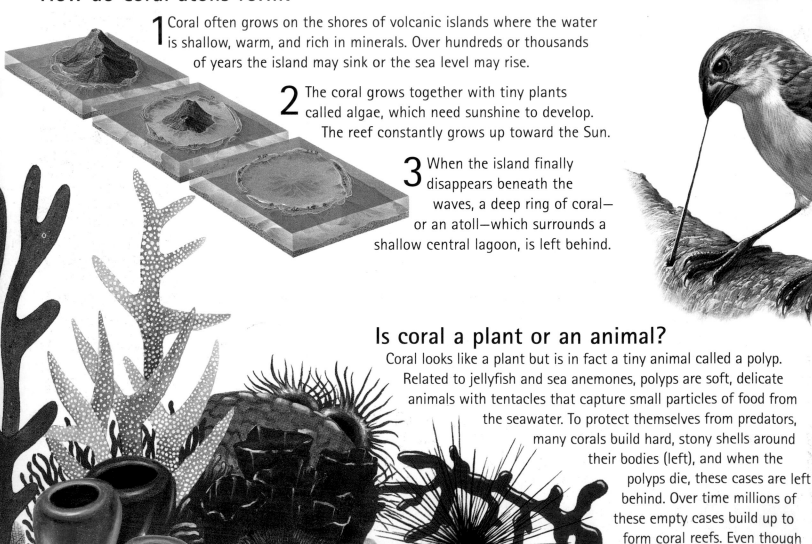

Is coral a plant or an animal?

Coral looks like a plant but is in fact a tiny animal called a polyp. Related to jellyfish and sea anemones, polyps are soft, delicate animals with tentacles that capture small particles of food from the seawater. To protect themselves from predators, many corals build hard, stony shells around their bodies (left), and when the polyps die, these cases are left behind. Over time millions of these empty cases build up to form coral reefs. Even though the bottom of a reef may be dead, the surface is very alive.

How do volcanoes form islands?

Underwater volcanoes are formed when magma forces its way through weak spots in the ocean's crust. When the lava meets the cold water, it solidifies. Over time this rock builds up, forming an undersea volcano. If the volcano grows big enough, its surface breaks off, and an island is born. The Galapagos Islands, the Hawaiian Islands, and the island of Surtsey, which appeared in the North Atlantic Ocean off the coast of Iceland in 1963, were all formed this way. When a volcanic island erupts, it can cause huge waves called tsunamis (left).

Which is the largest coral reef?

Off the east coast of Australia, stretching over 1,240 mi. (2,000km), the Great Barrier Reef is the biggest coral reef in the world. It is also the largest structure made by any living thing—it is so big it can be seen from space! Corals only grow about 6 in. (15cm) every year, making parts of the Great Barrier Reef approximately 18 million years old.

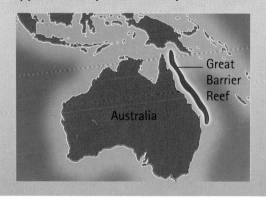

Australia
Great Barrier Reef

Why is island wildlife so special?

Islands may form in different ways, but they all have one thing in common—they are relatively isolated. As a result, they are often home to unusual animals that are found nowhere else. The unique ways in which finches developed on the Galapagos Islands—the woodpecker finch uses cactus thorns to spear insects (left)—helped Darwin develop his theory of evolution.

Why are coral reefs so rich in wildlife?

One third of all types of fish live on coral reefs, which are rivaled only by rain forests for their biodiversity—the variety of nature in them. In the warm, sunny waters of the reef food is plentiful, and the nooks and crannies provide shelter for both predators and prey. Large reefs are also millions of years old, allowing time for a complex web of life to develop.

Ocean Currents

Ocean currents are like huge rivers of water that flow through the sea, either at or near the surface or far below, close to the seabed. They are driven by wind and differences in water density and are affected by the depth and shape of the seabed and the spin of Earth. One of the largest currents—the West Wind Drift—carries 2,000 times more water than the Amazon River, the largest river in the world. Ocean currents have an important influence on climate and ocean transportation.

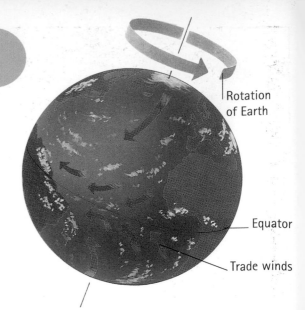

Rotation of Earth

Equator

Trade winds

What is the Coriolis effect?

Named after the French mathematician Gustave Coriolis, the Coriolis effect is produced by the rotation of Earth and has a direct bearing on wind and ocean-current patterns. Because Earth is spinning counterclockwise, winds and ocean currents traveling from either Pole to the equator are deflected significantly to the West (above).

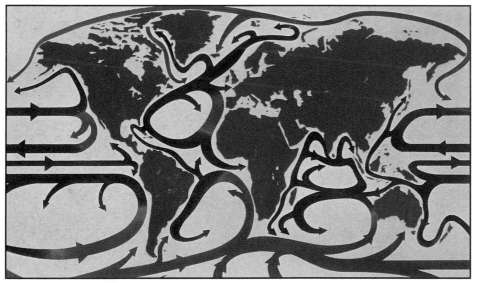

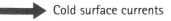 Cold surface currents  Warm surface currents

What do ocean currents carry?

Ocean currents once carried little more than unusual plant life. While seeds from South America still turn up in the U.K.—due to a current called the Gulf Stream—most debris comes from humans (below). Debris can sometimes provide valuable information about the speed and direction of currents. When 80,000 pairs of sneakers were swept off a ship traveling between South Korea and Seattle, an international study monitored when and where they finally washed up.

What causes surface currents?

Currents in the top 1,640 ft. (500m) of the ocean are called surface currents. They are caused by the wind and usually travel at about 6.2 mi. (10km) a day. They are deflected by the spin of Earth, which makes them flow clockwise in the Northern Hemisphere and counterclockwise in the Southern Hemisphere. Cold currents flowing from the polar regions replace warm currents pushed away from the tropical equatorial regions (above). Earth's spin, together with the shapes of the continents, makes the surface currents flow in five gigantic loops called gyres.

What are deep ocean currents?

In the polar oceans cold, very salty water sinks to the ocean floor and flows along the seabed toward the equator as a deep ocean current. As it warms up it becomes lighter than the surrounding water, so it rises to the surface. It then flows back to the Poles again as a warm surface current. This circular movement of water (left) means that eventually all the water in the oceans will relocate—but it can take 1,000 years for deep-sea water to return to the surface.

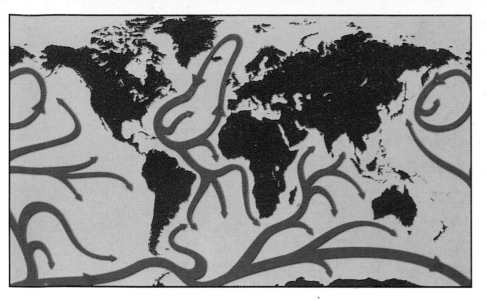

What is El Niño?

Off the coast of Peru, South America, cold water usually rises up from the ocean depths, bringing with it a rich supply of nutrients that provides food for millions of fish and birds. Every two to ten years, however, the winds change, and a warm water current called El Niño shifts the cold, nutritious current. With their food supply cut off, huge numbers of fish and seabirds die. El Niño also disrupts the weather, frequently causing serious flooding in Ecuador and Peru.

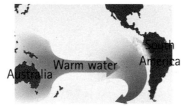

El Niño

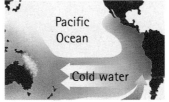

Normal conditions

How have ocean currents helped ocean explorers?

In 1947 the Norwegian explorer Thor Heyerdahl sailed a balsa-wood raft called *Kon-Tiki* from Peru to the Tuamotu Islands in eastern Polynesia. During a voyage that lasted four months the raft covered 7,022 mi. (11,300km), using the South Equatorial Current to help it on its way. Heyerdahl hoped that his adventure would prove that early South Americans could have reached the Polynesian Islands long before settlers arrived from the West.

Quick-fire Quiz

1. Which ocean current carries more water than the Amazon River?
a) El Niño
b) West Wind Drift
c) Gulf Stream

2. How far do surface currents usually travel in a single day?
a) 6.2 mi. (10km)
b) 62 mi. (100km)
c) 620 mi. (1,000km)

3. What temperature is the El Niño current?
a) Cold
b) Warm
c) Icy

4. How long does it take for a deep ocean current to resurface?
a) 10 years
b) 100 years
c) 1,000 years

Oceans and Climate

The oceans have a major effect on Earth's climate, soaking up the Sun's warmth and carrying heat from the equator toward the Poles using ocean currents. Winds blowing over the oceans are warmed up or cooled down by the water, and these winds then raise or lower temperatures on the land. The oceans also release huge amounts of moisture into the air, which may later fall as rain or snow.

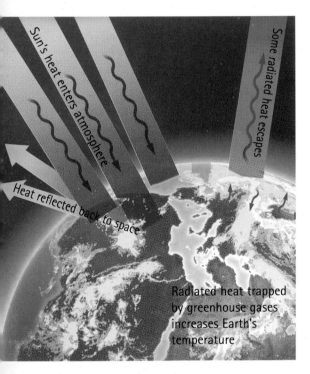

Sun's heat enters atmosphere

Some radiated heat escapes

Heat reflected back to space

Radiated heat trapped by greenhouse gases increases Earth's temperature

Are sea levels rising?

Sea levels rise and fall as Earth's temperature increases or decreases. Warmer temperatures cause the ocean waters to expand and some of the polar ice caps to melt, making sea levels rise. This is because sea levels are related to the amount of water trapped in snow and ice. Because of global warming, caused by the greenhouse effect (left), sea levels are rising—and by the year 2100 they may have risen by 18 in. (45cm). Such an increase would drown hundreds of coral atolls and threaten cities such as New York.

What is a hurricane?

Fierce, whirling storms called hurricanes can be up to 370 mi. (600km) wide, with destructive winds spinning up to 105 mph (170km/h). Hurricanes start over oceans near the equator, where two air masses meet and the ocean temperature is at least 77°F (25°C). Warm, moist air is drawn up from the ocean's surface in a slow, circular motion caused by Earth's rotation. The hurricane draws more and more warm air up—making the storm grow. Over land the storm is cut off from the warm air that drives it and eventually loses its power.

What is a waterspout?

A waterspout is a whirling tornado that forms over warm, tropical waters, such as those in the Gulf of Mexico. Unlike a hurricane, which grows from the surface of the sea up, a waterspout begins as a rotating funnel of air extending down from a thundercloud (right). As it touches the surface of the sea, water is sucked up to form a column that can extend 33 ft. (10m) across and can be up to 400 ft. (120m) high.

Why is San Francisco usually foggy?

Sea fog forms when warm, moist air moves over cold water, causing the vapor in the air to condense into a fine mist. The California Current off the coast of San Francisco carries cold water south from the Arctic Ocean. When warm, moist air moves over this water, a dense fog forms—shrouding the city and its famous Golden Gate Bridge (above).

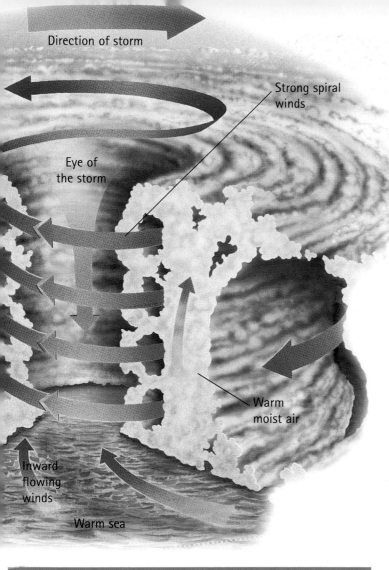

Direction of storm

Strong spiral winds

Eye of the storm

Warm moist air

Inward flowing winds

Warm sea

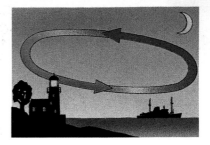

What are land and sea breezes?

Coastal winds that blow onto the land during the day and out to sea at night are called land and sea breezes. They occur because the sea warms up and cools down slower than the land. On a sunny day (above left), the land heats up faster than the sea, so warm air rises off the land, and a cool breeze is sucked in from the sea. If the night is clear (above right), the land cools down faster than the sea. As warm air rises over the sea it draws the cooler, land air out over the water.

What is the Thames Barrier?

The Thames Barrier in London, England, can seal off the upper part of the Thames River from the sea—protecting the city from storm surges and very high tides. The barrier consists of ten movable gates, each as high as a five-story building, supported between concrete piers. The gates usually lie flat on the riverbed, but they can be rotated 90 degrees up at the first sign of dangerously high water.

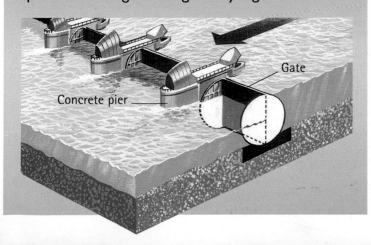

Concrete pier

Gate

What are fjords?

About 10,000 years ago, during the last Ice Age, glaciers carved out long, deep valleys along the coasts of countries such as Norway. As the ice melted and sea levels rose these U-shaped glacial valleys were flooded to form long, steep-sided inlets called fjords (below).

Quick-fire Quiz

1. Which country has a lot of fjords?
a) India
b) Norway
c) Australia

2. How many gates does the Thames Barrier have?
a) 5
b) 10
c) 12

3. What affects sea levels most?
a) Earth's temperature
b) The Sun
c) The moon

4. Where do hurricanes form?
a) Over warm, tropical oceans
b) Over cold, polar oceans
c) In the North Sea

Waves and Tides

Most waves are caused by the wind. The faster the wind and the longer it blows, the larger the waves. Volcanic eruptions or earthquakes can also produce destructive waves that reach 100 ft. (30m) high. The more gentle, everyday rising and falling of the tides is caused by the pull of gravity from the moon and the Sun. The highest tides occur in the Bay of Fundy, Canada, where the sea can rise higher than a four-story building in just six hours.

How do waves work?

Unlike currents and tides, waves do not move water along. The waves travel, but the water within each wave stays in almost the same place—moving around in circles. Long after the wind that created them has died away, waves can travel huge distances. Waves that break off the coast of California may have begun 6,215 mi. (10,000km) away.

Water moves in circles

Waves break in shallow water

What causes tides?

On most coasts the sea rises and falls twice a day. High tide is when the water is "in," and low tide is when the water is "out." Tides are caused mainly by the pull of the moon's gravity. The moon pulls the water in the oceans nearest to it out. At the same time, because Earth is spinning, the oceans on the opposite side of Earth are also pulled out. These two bulges in Earth's oceans correspond to high tides, while the oceans in between are at low tide. Tides change (rise or fall) as Earth spins and the position of the moon alters.

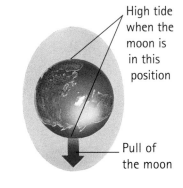

High tide when the moon is in this position

Pull of the moon

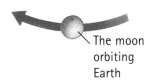

The moon orbiting Earth

What happens to waves when they reach the shore?

As a wave nears the shore the sea is too shallow for the water inside it to make a circle, so the crest of the wave topples over and the wave breaks—releasing the energy stored up during its journey. Surfers (left) try to stay just ahead of this breaking crest. If the seabed slopes gently, waves break before reaching the shore; where it is steeper, the waves surge onto the shore. The foaming water that rushes up the beach is called swash, and the water returning to the sea is called backwash.

What are spring and neap tides?

The Sun's pull on Earth's oceans is weak because it is so far away. But twice a month, when the Sun, the moon, and Earth are in line (below left), the pulls of the Sun and the moon combine to produce higher high tides and lower low tides than usual. These spring tides happen during the full and the new moons. When the Sun, the moon, and Earth form a right angle (below right), the Sun's pull works against the moon, producing lower high tides and higher low tides. These neap tides happen when the moon is in its first and last quarter.

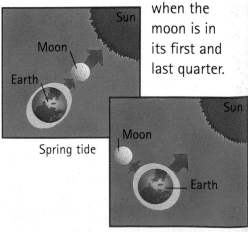

Sun

Moon

Earth

Spring tide

Sun

Moon

Earth

Neap tide

How can waves and tides generate electricity?

Water is a valuable source of energy. On coasts where the tidal range is over 16 ft. (5m) a tidal barrage, or barrier, harnesses the energy in waves to rock huge floats. These floats absorb the energy and use it to drive pumps. The pumps force liquid through turbines, which generate electricity.

What is a tsunami?

Waves that are triggered by undersea volcanoes or earthquakes are called tsunamis. These are far more powerful than the waves produced by the wind—tsunamis cause all the water from the seabed to the surface of the sea to move. In the open ocean these waves appear small, but they travel huge distances at the speed of a jet. When they approach land, they slow down and grow into a terrifying wall of water 100–160 ft. (30–50m) high (below). The largest recorded tsunamis have been over than 920 ft. (280m) high.

How do waves and tides affect wildlife?

Waves can pound, crush, or uproot shore creatures from their hiding places. Tides expose them to predators, such as birds (below), and to the Sun and wind. So, animals that live on the shore must be resourceful. Some burrow beneath the sand for safety, while others hide in tidal pools or among the rocks. Many have special features, such as the cone-shaped, wave-resistant shells of limpets.

Quick-fire Quiz

1. What is the main cause of ocean tides?
a) The moon's gravity
b) The Sun's gravity
c) Earth's rotation

2. What are spring tides?
a) Higher and lower tides than usual
b) Tides that happen in the spring
c) Tides that come in really quickly

3. What causes a tsunami?
a) An undersea volcano or earthquake
b) Very strong winds
c) Hurricanes

4. Which animal has a cone-shaped shell to help it resist the waves?
a) Mussel
b) Clam
c) Limpet

Coasts

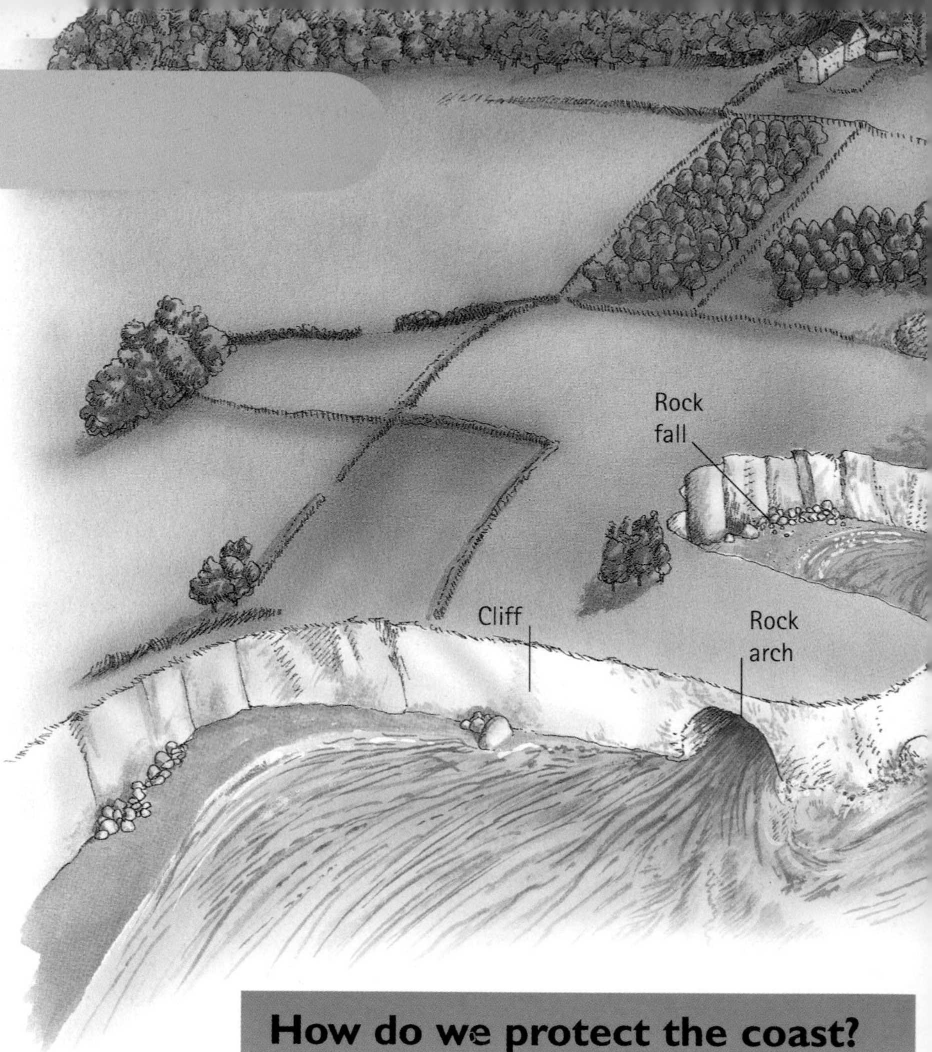

The world's coastlines stretch for about 310,695 mi. (500,000km)—long enough to circle the equator 12 times. Despite this great length almost every coastline is different. This is because the shape of the coast depends on the kind of rock it is made of and how it is shaped by the waves and the wind. Some coasts are steadily being added to, while others are being eroded by the relentless action of the wind and waves.

Rock fall

Cliff

Rock arch

What lives in tidal pools?

Safely hidden underwater in a tidal pool (below), a wide variety of coastal wildlife can wait for the high tide. Sea anemones and shellfish cling to the rocks, while crabs, shrimps, and prawns scuttle about, and sea urchins scrape away at plants with their powerful teeth. Tidal pools can be difficult places to live in. Exposed to the Sun, wind, and rain, the temperature, acidity, and saltiness of the water can vary enormously. Oxygen and carbon dioxide levels can also fluctuate, with often disastrous consequences for the pool's inhabitants.

How do we protect the coast?

About 60 percent of the world's population lives within 35 mi. (60km) of the coast, and over two thirds of the world's cities, with populations over one million, are by the sea. Huge numbers of tourists also take vacations at the coast. Many coastlines are protected by sea walls, breakwaters, and artificial beaches. But natural coastlines are constantly changing, and when we try to protect the coast and keep beaches from being washed away, it often causes problems at a different point along the coast.

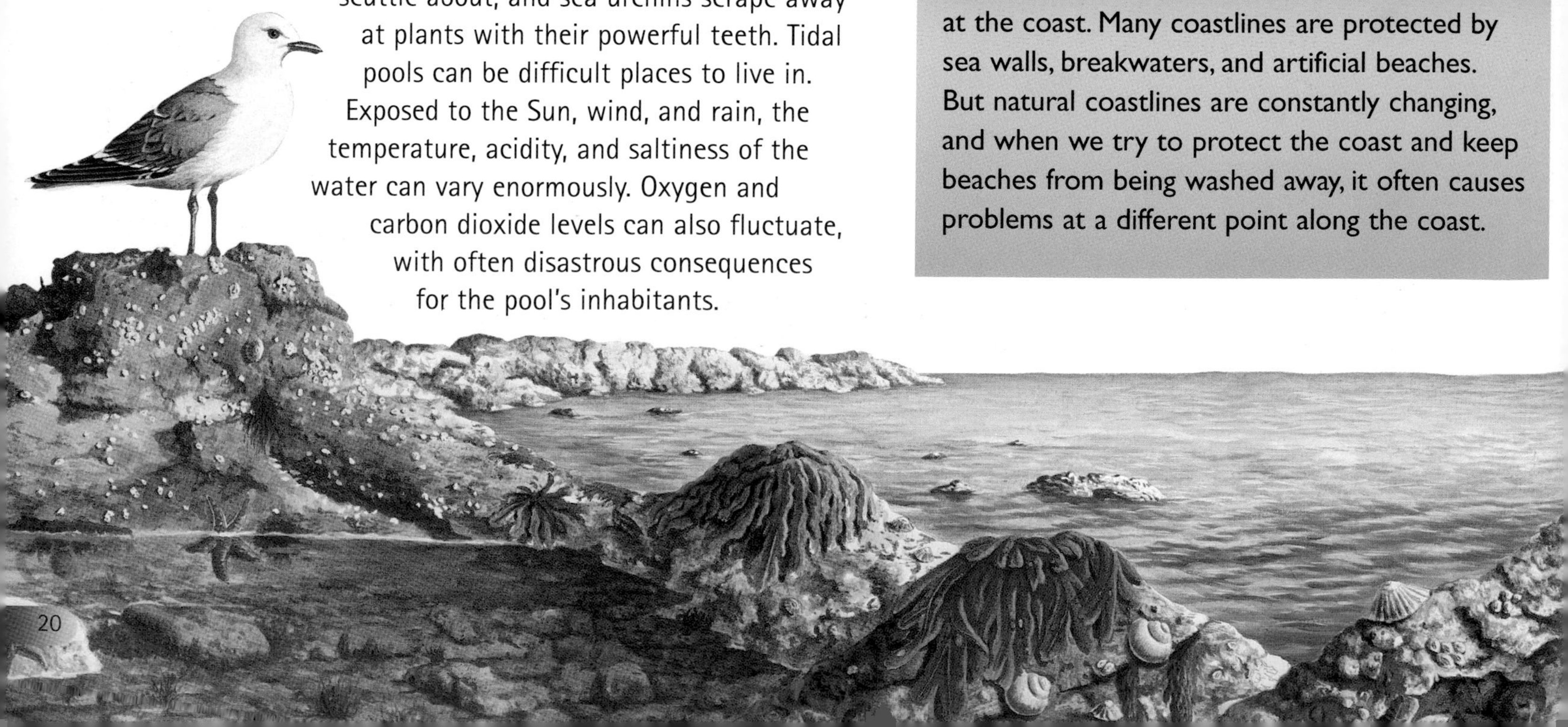

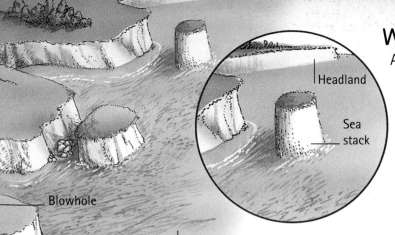

What is a sea stack?

A tall pillar of rock just off the coast is called a sea stack (left). It starts to form when waves cut away caves on both sides of a headland. Eventually the caves meet in the middle, and a rock arch is formed. The waves continue to lap around the arch, steadily widening it until the roof collapses and an isolated sea stack remains.

How do waves wear away the coast?

The main way in which the sea wears away, or erodes, a coast is by hurling sand and pebbles against it. The sheer force of the waves also helps break the rocks up into smaller pieces. In places where the coast is being eroded by the sea there are bays, cliffs, and headlands (left). The world's highest sea cliffs are in Hawaii. They are over twice the height of the Empire State Building in New York City!

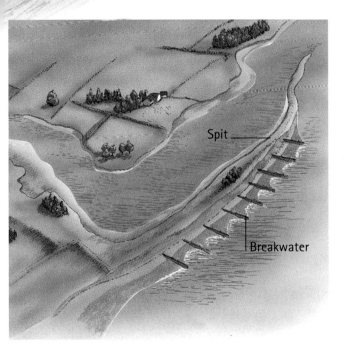

What is a spit?

When a coastline curves or changes direction, longshore drift (below) may wash sand and gravel out to sea— forming a long, snakelike ridge called a spit (left). The tip of a spit often curves toward the land because the waves push beach materials in that direction. If a spit grows across the mouth of a bay, it may eventually reach the mainland on the other side— cutting off the bay from the open ocean. The spit is then called a bay barrier. If an island is joined to the mainland by a spit, the spit is called a tombolo.

What is longshore drift?

On some coasts the sand or gravel is moved along the shore by the waves (right). This is called longshore drift, and it happens when the waves hit the beach at an angle before falling back down the beach in a straight line. As the waves follow this zig-zag path along the coast they take some of the beach with them. Sea walls called breakwaters are often built to trap the sand and stop it from drifting away.

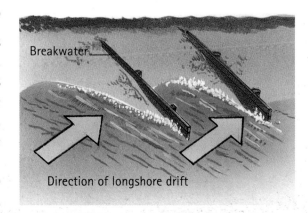

Breakwater

Direction of longshore drift

Quick-fire Quiz

1. What is the name of a spit that joins an island to the mainland?
a) A causeway
b) A bay barrier
c) A tombolo

2. What is the name for the walls built to stop longshore drift?
a) Breakwaters
b) Piers
c) Sea walls

3. Where are the world's highest sea cliffs found?
a) The Orkney Islands
b) Hawaii
c) California

4. Which animals cling to the rocks in tidal pools?
a) Shrimps and prawns
b) Crabs and lobsters
c) Sea anemones and shellfish

A River's Journey

Rivers contain less than one percent of all the freshwater on Earth, yet they are a powerful force in shaping the land. Over thousands of years rivers can wear away the rocks they flow over, and carve out broad, flat-bottomed valleys. They also carry away rocks, sand, and sediment, depositing them in lakes, under the sea, or on the land, making rich farming soil.

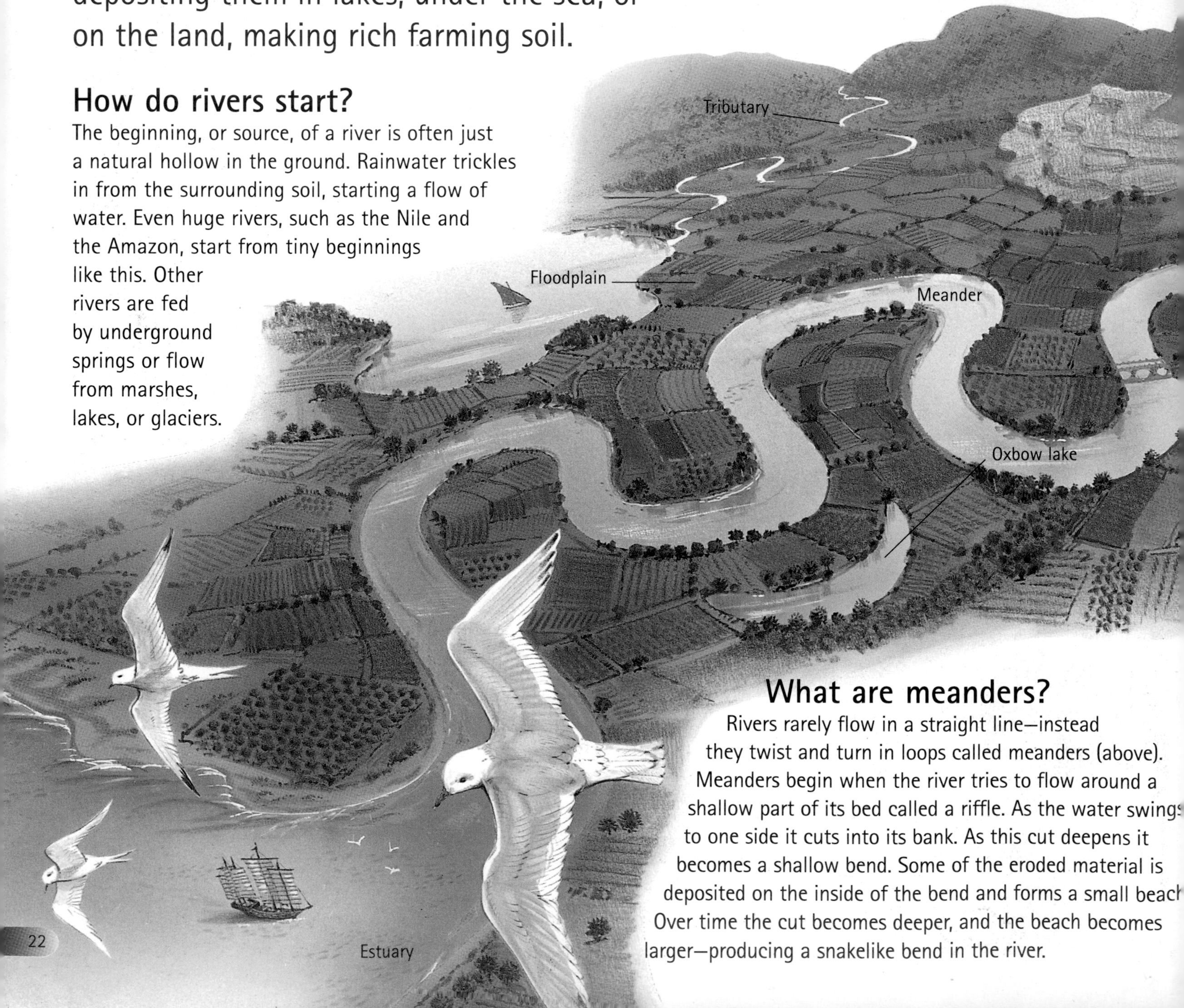

How do rivers start?

The beginning, or source, of a river is often just a natural hollow in the ground. Rainwater trickles in from the surrounding soil, starting a flow of water. Even huge rivers, such as the Nile and the Amazon, start from tiny beginnings like this. Other rivers are fed by underground springs or flow from marshes, lakes, or glaciers.

Tributary

Floodplain

Meander

Oxbow lake

Estuary

What are meanders?

Rivers rarely flow in a straight line—instead they twist and turn in loops called meanders (above). Meanders begin when the river tries to flow around a shallow part of its bed called a riffle. As the water swings to one side it cuts into its bank. As this cut deepens it becomes a shallow bend. Some of the eroded material is deposited on the inside of the bend and forms a small beach. Over time the cut becomes deeper, and the beach becomes larger—producing a snakelike bend in the river.

How do rivers wear away the land?

Rivers usually cut into the land using abrasion—they scratch and scrape at the riverbeds with the rocks and sediments that they carry. Where the river water swirls pebbles around in circles, potholes may form on the riverbed. Rivers are most powerful in flood conditions when the increased volume of water sweeps huge amounts of soil and large rocks downstream. Rivers can also dissolve some rocks and carry them away in their waters.

Rain falls on high ground

River begins as small mountain stream

Rivers join as they flow to the sea

How is an oxbow lake formed?

Oxbow lake

River

Once a river has begun to meander, the snakelike curves steadily become more extreme as the water swings powerfully into the outside of the bend and drops sediment on the inner side of the river's path. Over time the neck of a meander can become narrow. If the river floods, it may cut through this neck, leaving the meander behind as an oxbow lake.

Quick-fire Quiz

1. What is the shallow part of a riverbed called?
a) A rapid
b) A riffle
c) A weir

2. Which lake is one of the sources of the Nile River?
a) Lake Superior
b) Lake Margaret
c) Lake Victoria

3. How much shorter than the Nile is the Amazon?
a) 370 mi. (596km)
b) 423 mi. (680km)
c) 158 mi. (255km)

4. What kind of lake is formed from a meandering river?
a) An oxtail lake
b) A horseshoe lake
c) An oxbow lake

How is the otter adapted to live in rivers?

The otter is an excellent swimmer with webbed feet, a streamlined body, and a muscular tail for steering through the water. When swimming slowly, it uses a kind of doggy paddle. But by flexing its whole body up and down like a seal, the otter can reach speeds of up to 6.2 mph (10km/h). To stay warm and dry in even the coldest rivers, the otter has two layers of fur. The outer layer of guard hairs is waterproof, while a dense, fine underfur traps air, keeping the otter warm.

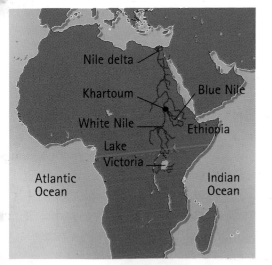

Nile delta

Khartoum

Blue Nile

White Nile

Ethiopia

Lake Victoria

Atlantic Ocean

Indian Ocean

Which is the world's longest river?

Flowing 4,160 mi. (6,695km) through northeast Africa, the Nile (left) is the world's longest river. The Amazon River is a close second, being just 158 mi. (255km) shorter. The Nile has two main sources—the White Nile, which flows from Lake Victoria, and the Blue Nile, which flows from the Ethiopian highlands. The White and Blue Nile rivers join at Khartoum in Sudan, and from there the river flows north to the Mediterranean Sea, where it ends in a vast triangular delta. Much of the river's course is through desert, where it brings life to the parched landscape.

River Landscapes

A river is said to have a youth, middle age, and old age. According to its age, it changes the landscape in different ways (right). In its youth, near its source, it races over waterfalls and rapids, carving out a deep valley. Downstream, in middle age, it slows down, losing its cutting power—it begins to meander, or wander, spilling onto a plain during floods. In old age the river widens as it nears the sea, forming an estuary, and the flow slows down.

Floodplain

Meander

Floodplain

Estuary

What are river canyons?

Some rivers carve out long, deep valleys called canyons—especially where the climate is very dry. Here rain falls in sharp, heavy bursts. There is little soil and few plants to soak up the water, so it rushes over the land, cutting down with great force. The Grand Canyon (left), a famous river canyon, is over 280 mi. (450km) long and about 1 mi. (1.5km) deep.

Why are river valleys V-shaped?

Close to a river's source its valley is narrow and steep-sided (left). This is because the fast-flowing water sweeps along pebbles and grit, which act as powerful abrasives. In this way the river cuts down faster than it cuts sideways, and so it makes a V shape.

Waterfall

Rapids

What is a drainage pattern?

The way that rivers and streams all join up in an area is called a drainage pattern, and there are several different types. A dendritic drainage pattern, for example, looks like the branches of a tree—the Amazon River has this kind of drainage pattern (right). Some other patterns are called radial, trellis, and parallel patterns.

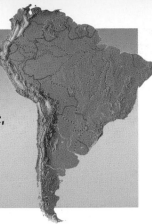

Where is the highest waterfall in the world?

The highest waterfall is Angel Falls (right) in Venezuela, South America. Here water from the Carrao River plunges over a sheer cliff for 2,648 ft. (807m) in a single drop before hitting a rocky outcrop. It then tumbles a further 565 ft. (172m) before hitting the base, giving a total drop of 3,213 ft. (979m)—more than three times the height of the Eiffel Tower!

What is a floodplain?

A floodplain (above) is a wide, flat valley near the end of a river's course. Here it is easy for a river to break its banks in times of flooding, spilling water and mud over the floodplain and creating good soil for farming (left).

Eiffel Tower
985 ft. (300m)

Quick-fire Quiz

1. Which letter of the alphabet is the same shape as a river valley?
a) W
b) V
c) U

2. What does dendritic drainage look like?
a) Tree branches
b) Wheel spokes
c) A triangle

3. What is a floodplain?
a) A deep, narrow valley
b) A stretch of fast-flowing water
c) A wide, flat valley floor

4. What kinds of rocks do waterfalls form over?
a) Hard rocks
b) Soft rocks
c) Strips of hard and soft rocks

How is a waterfall made?

1 When a river flows over strips of hard and soft rock, the soft rock wears away first, leaving a slight step.

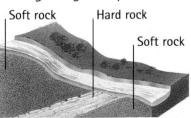

Soft rock   Hard rock

Soft rock

2 The soft rock below the step wears away faster because the water falls with greater force onto it.

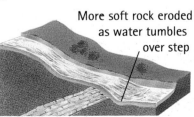

More soft rock eroded as water tumbles over step

3 In time the water cuts out a deep pool below the hard rock step. Now the water has to fall over the lip of the step.

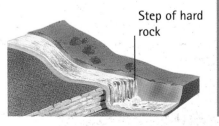

Step of hard rock

Where Rivers Meet the Sea

Delta shape

Arcuate delta

Most rivers end their long journey at the sea. Here the river's flow slows down, and the heavy load of sediment is finally allowed to settle. On the coast, if the tides are strong enough, some of this sediment is washed out to sea. But some of it may build up into a new piece of land called a delta. This word comes from "Δ," the symbol for the Greek letter "d," which is the same triangular shape. Many rivers, however, simply end in broad stretches of water called estuaries.

What shape are deltas?

The shape of a delta depends on how much water and sediment is carried by the river and how fast it is flowing. It also depends on the speed and strength of the waves, currents, and tides on the coast. An arcuate delta (above), such as that of the Nile, Indus, or Rhône rivers, forms where waves, currents, and tides are weak. A cuspate delta, like that of Italy's Tiber River, ends in a point or peak. Here strong waves force the sediment to spread out in both directions from the river's mouth. A bird's-foot delta, like that of the Mississippi River, forms when a lot of sediment is carried out into calm seawater.

Lake

Estuary

Sea

What is a river estuary?

An estuary is the broad area of water where a river meets the sea (right). It is a place of constant change. At low tide it is a freshwater environment, but at high tide it becomes increasingly salty. Estuaries are also muddy places because the river slows down as it meets the sea and releases the sediment it is carrying. The seawater makes the mud and silt clump together and drift to the bottom. Huge numbers of worms and shellfish live in this rich mud, providing food for many birds.

Why do flounders have both eyes on one side?

Flounders (right) are a type of fish that have developed flattened bodies so that they can lie hidden among the sand and silt on the riverbed or seabed. Because they lie on one side, they have both eyes on the other—usually the right side. When they start life, however, they look like most other fish, with one eye on either side of their head. As they grow, one eye moves to the same side of the head as the other eye. The nostril and the mouth also move to this side of the head. Flounders are typical estuary fish, migrating upriver to feed in the summer and returning to the sea to breed in the fall.

Why are mangroves unusual?

Mangrove trees are unusual because they have adapted to life in wet, salty, and muddy swamps. Their stiltlike, arching roots (left) trap mud brought down to the sea by rivers and help transform coastal swamps into dry land. They grow so densely that they help protect the coast from storms and floods. Mangroves are also odd because they "breathe" air through their arching roots. They need to do this because there is very little oxygen in the wet mud. The seeds that mangroves produce start to grow on the tree, which increases their chance of survival when they drop into the mud below.

Why is quicksand dangerous?

Quicksand is usually found in hollows at the mouth of large rivers or along flat stretches of sandy beach. It forms where a permanent pool of water becomes filled up with sand and sediment. The sand is so waterlogged that it cannot support any weight, and so it behaves like a liquid. If a person steps onto an area of quicksand, they may be sucked beneath the surface and eventually drown.

Which fish is good at skipping?

Mudskippers (right) are finger-sized fish that live in mangrove swamps and mudflats all around the Indian and Pacific oceans, from Africa to Polynesia. Whenever the tide goes out, they wriggle their tails and skip across the mud or climb mangrove trees using their stumpy fins. When they are out of the water, they breathe air that is held within their gill chambers. Some mudskippers claim territories, building low mud walls that keep their rivals out and prevent seawater from draining away at low tide.

Lakes

Lakes are water-filled hollows, varying in size, in the surface of the land. Most of these hollows were carved out by huge glaciers and ice sheets, but some were formed by movements deep inside Earth's crust. Rivers sometimes become lakes when they come up against a barrier that acts like a dam.

Which lakes are formed by Earth's movements?

The world's deepest lakes were formed by movements and volcanic activity beneath Earth's crust, or skin, that caused the crust to crumple or crack. In some places deep cracking of the crust caused huge blocks of land to drop below the level of the surrounding land, creating steep-sided valleys called rift valleys. Over time water filled up parts of the valleys, creating long, deep rift lakes (left).

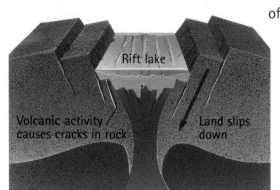

Rift lake

Volcanic activity causes cracks in rock

Land slips down

What are the Great Lakes?

The five large lakes (Superior, Michigan, Huron, Erie, and Ontario) between the border of the U.S. and Canada are called the Great Lakes (inset left). The water from Lake Erie plunges over the Niagara Falls before reaching Lake Ontario. Lake Superior is the second largest body of inland water in the world—after the Caspian Sea—and the largest and deepest of the Great Lakes. Its surface area, at more than 31,700 sq. mi. (82,000 sq km), is almost double the entire size of Switzerland (inset left). Lake Superior is so large that the wind whips across its surface over great distances and forms huge waves, which produce sealike conditions. Large ships (left) carry goods to and from the many ports on the Great Lakes.

Switzerland

CANADA
Lake Superior
Lake Huron
Lake Michigan
Lake Ontario
Lake Erie
U.S.

What are volcanic lakes?

Volcanic activity can form lakes in many ways. A lake may be formed when the solidified core, or plug, of an old volcano sinks down below the crater's rim, forming a hollow called a caldera. If the caldera fills up with water, it is called a crater lake. The largest caldera in the world is in Sumatra, Indonesia, and contains Lake Toba. Other lakes form when volcanic debris or lava dams a river, and the water collects behind the dam to form a lake. Some volcanic lakes, such as Kawah Idjen (right) in Java, Indonesia, have a high level of powerful acids in their water. Acidic gases bubble up through cracks on the bottom of the lake from the volcano below and dissolve in the water. Living things cannot survive in such highly acidic water, and people can be badly burned if they touch it.

Which lake is the deepest?

Lake Baikal (inset right) in Siberia plunges to 5,370 ft. (1,637m) and is the world's deepest lake. Its surface area is the sixth largest in the world. Lake Baikal contains around one fifth of all the unfrozen freshwater on Earth—336 rivers and streams flow into it. During the Siberian winter parts of the lake freeze over, and local people use the ice as a highway (right). There is a huge variety of wildlife in the lake—three quarters of the species are found nowhere else on Earth, including the Baikal seal—the world's only freshwater seal.

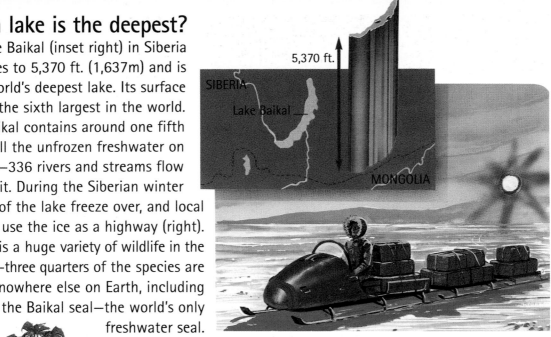

5,370 ft.

SIBERIA

Lake Baikal

MONGOLIA

Quick-fire Quiz

1. When was the last Ice Age?
a) 1 million years ago
b) 18,000 years ago
c) 5,000 years ago

2. How are the world's deepest lakes formed?
a) By glaciers
b) By Earth's movements
c) By beavers

3. How many rivers flow into Lake Baikal?
a) 400
b) 336
c) 556

4. How many Great Lakes are there?
a) 5
b) 9
c) 16

What are swamps and marshes?

A swamp is a cross between a lake and land. Its waters are usually very shallow and still, and yet many special kinds of trees and plants can be found growing in the water. The Everglades in Florida is an enormous swamp, covering 4,093 sq. mi. (10,600 sq km). A marsh is drier than a swamp, and water cannot always be seen there, but the ground and the plants that grow in it are always soggy or heavily waterlogged. A marsh rarely has any trees.

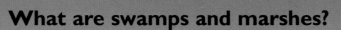

Swamp

Marsh

Which lakes are formed by the action of glaciers?

About 18,000 years ago, during the last Ice Age, ice sheets and glaciers covered much larger areas of land than they do now. As the ice moved over the land it carved out great dips in the ground. When the climate warmed up and the ice melted, water filled in these dips to form lakes, such as the lochs of Scotland. High up in the mountains, circular hollows called cirques (right), which were scraped out by the huge weight of ice at the head of glaciers, filled up with water and became lakes. Other lakes formed when debris left behind by melting glaciers formed dams, sometimes trapping water behind them.

Cirque

Head of glacier

Water Under the Ground

When rain falls, some of it runs straight into rivers and lakes—but most of it soaks through the soil to the rocks below. If the rocks will not let the rain pass through (permeate), an underground river may form, flowing on top of the rocks. Where the rain can flow through the rocks, pockets of water called aquifers develop. Over time soft rocks, such as limestone, can be worn away by this water, and huge tunnels and caves may form.

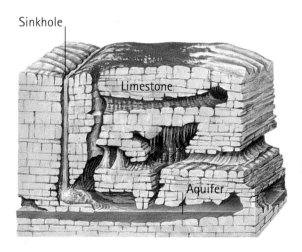

Sinkhole

Limestone

Aquifer

What are stalactites and stalagmites?

As water drips down from the roof of a limestone cave it dissolves the minerals in the rocks. Some of the water in the drops evaporates, leaving the minerals behind. Over hundreds of years these build up into icicle-shaped stalactites, which hang down from cave roofs (right). Stalagmites build up from water drops that splash onto the floor of the cave. Sometimes a stalactite and a stalagmite meet in the middle and form a pillar.

What is an aquifer?

An aquifer is a layer of rock or sediment through which water moves easily. Good aquifer materials include sandstone, chalk, and limestone. These rocks are said to be porous because there are tiny gaps, or pores, between the grains of rock through which water can flow. Some aquifers have been filling up for thousands of years and are like huge underground reservoirs. Wells are often drilled into these rocks, and the water is pumped out, although ancient aquifers can dry out quickly.

What is an artesian well?

Sometimes an aquifer is sandwiched in a basin between two layers of impermeable rock—rock that will not allow water to pass through it. Because of the weight of the water pushing down from the sides of the basin, the base of the aquifer is under pressure. If a well is dug out here, the water will gush out by itself. This is called an artesian well—the first well of this kind was dug by the Romans in Artesium, France.

Rain

Aquifer

Artesian well

Impermeable rock

Impermeable rock

How do caves and caverns form?

Cracks in limestone rock may be widened by rainwater, leaving a deep, vertical shaft called a sinkhole or a swallow hole. Water may flow down the sides of the hole to form spectacular underground waterfalls, often hundreds of feet deep. Underground water also dissolves limestone rock to form caves and caverns (left). Cave explorers enter these caves by climbing down large sinkholes called potholes. The longest cave system in the world lies under Mammoth Cave National Park in Kentucky. It is over 330 mi. (530km) long and has more than 60,000 sinkholes.

What makes a geyser gush?

A geyser is a type of hot spring that regularly shoots out spectacular fountains of water and steam. Geysers occur in volcanic areas where hot rocks lie near the surface. The rocks heat underground water to the boiling point. As the water boils its pressure rises, forcing the cooler water above it into a column up to 1,640 ft. (500m) tall (right). Some geysers, such as Old Faithful in Yellowstone National Park, erupt every hour or so. Other geysers may wait weeks or months between eruptions.

How does an oasis form?

An oasis is a moist, fertile area of a desert where an aquifer is close to the surface. The water often comes from rain that falls on mountains hundreds of miles away before draining below the desert surface. A fault, or crack, above the aquifer (left) may allow this water to reach the surface naturally, or a well may sometimes be dug to deliberately create an oasis.

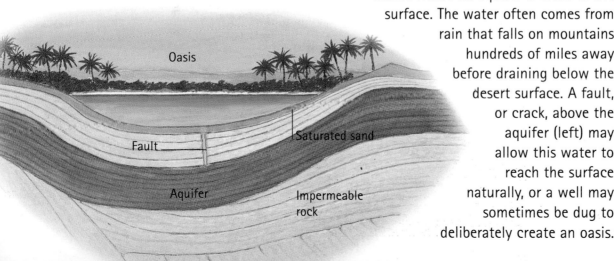

Oasis

Fault

Saturated sand

Aquifer

Impermeable rock

People, Oceans, and Rivers

People have always had a close relationship with
Earth's waters. Fish from the oceans have been a
valuable food source for thousands of years, and fresh
river water is vital for drinking, washing, and irrigating
our crops. People also use water for transportation,
trade, vacations, and water sports. The awesome
power of waves, tides, and fast-flowing rivers has
more recently been harnessed to give us electricity—
while oil and minerals are mined from the seabed.

Are fish frozen at sea?

Huge factory fishing ships (above) stay at
sea for months at a time and catch huge
amounts of fish. In one day they can catch
over 600 tons of fish, which have to be
preserved until the ship gets back to port.
First the fish are gutted, cleaned, and
filleted. The guts are turned into fish meal
or fish oil for fertilizers or animal feed
and stored in bags. The filleted fish are
compressed into blocks of seafood paste
and are quickly frozen and packaged. They
are then stored in a refrigerated
compartment. Nothing
is wasted!

How do people use water for irrigation?

Since the time of
the ancient Egyptians,
people have used various
devices to lift river water
onto their fields to water their
crops. In Egypt today farmers still
use the same simple but effective
devices, such as Archimedes' screw and
shadoof (left), which have been around for
thousands of years. Archimedes' screw is like
a corkscrew inside a tube. By turning the screw
many times a large amount of water can be
lifted with little effort. In many countries
low walls are built around fields to hold in
the water, and floodgates control the flow
to the fields. Today electric pumps are also
used to carry water from rivers to the fields.

Archimedes'
screw

Shadoof

Where does oil come from?

Oil comes from the remains of tiny sea creatures that once thrived in Earth's ancient oceans. Over millions of years, heat and pressure have changed their remains into oil. Today, although the pattern of land and sea is very different, about two fifths of our oil comes from under the sea. To bring it to the surface, huge drilling platforms are towed out to the edge of the continental shelf, where they drill wells 3,000–16,400 ft. (900–5,000m) into the seabed.

What pollutes the oceans?

Pollution has had a disastrous effect on many coastlines and land-locked seas. City sewage, chemical and industrial waste, and farmers' pesticides and fertilizers all find their way into Earth's seas and oceans. Out on the open ocean tons of waste and garbage is thoughtlessly thrown overboard from ships every day. But oil is one of the major pollutants of the oceans. It comes from ships illegally cleaning their oil tanks with seawater and from tragic accidents, such as when a tanker hits the ground and spills its load (right). Another threat to the health of our oceans comes from the radioactive pollution of coastal nuclear power plants and sunken or damaged nuclear submarines.

Quick-fire Quiz

1. How deep are most offshore oil wells?
a) 3,000–16,400 ft.
b) 330–1,640 ft.
c) 16,400–55,620 ft.

2. What is power generated from water called?
a) Aquaelectricity
b) Hydroelectricity
c) Turbine power

3. How much fish can a factory ship catch each day?
a) 400 tons
b) 600 tons
c) 800 tons

4. Where does oil come from?
a) From deep-sea vents
b) From the remains of tiny sea creatures
c) From ancient fossilized trees

Why do people dam rivers?

Dams are very strong, thick walls built across rivers to hold back the water (right). The water can then be released gradually to prevent flooding downstream. The water from the dam's reservoir can also be used to drive turbines and generate electricity. Such hydroelectric power plants do not pollute the environment and use a resource that will never run out. The only drawbacks are that a large area behind the dam must be flooded and changing the natural flow of water in a river can cause floods or droughts in other areas.

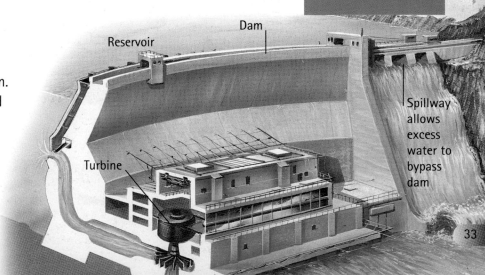

Dam

Reservoir

Spillway allows excess water to bypass dam

Turbine

33

Watercraft

People have sailed the seas and oceans since the earliest times. Their first ships were made of wood and powered by oars and sails. Much later metal ships with steam and diesel engines were built. Today there is an incredible variety of watercraft—from jet skis to enormous cargo ships. Some ships zoom across the ocean at high speeds, while nuclear submarines lurk far below.

How does a submarine dive and resurface?

A submarine dives underwater or rises to the surface by filling up large tanks with water or air. If the tanks are filled with water, the submarine becomes heavier than the water around it and sinks down. When it has reached its chosen depth, the valves that let water into the tanks are closed, and the submarine stays at that depth. For the submarine to resurface, air is pumped into the tanks—forcing the water out and making the submarine light enough to rise. Modern nuclear-powered submarines are totally self-contained, even recycling the air that the crew breathes. In this way they can stay submerged for as long as their food supplies last.

A submarine floats when its tanks are full of air

To dive the air is allowed to escape, and water fills the tanks

To rise air is pumped back into the tanks

What kinds of watercraft are used for water sports?

People take part in many water sports on rivers, lakes, and seas. Windsurfers zoom across the water on sailboards, while kayakers race their fiberglass kayaks through the surf or down white-water rapids. For those in search of speed, streamlined speedboats can travel incredibly fast. Some racing boats even have aircraft engines and have set world speed records. Jet skis first went on sale in Japan in 1979, and the latest models can zip along at speeds of up to 65 mph (105km/h).

K-153

What are container ships?

Container ships (below) carry all kinds of goods in large metal boxes called containers. Each container is a standard size—about 40 ft. (12m) long and 8 ft. (2.5m) wide, so they can easily be stacked on board the ship. Each ship holds many thousands of containers, which are loaded and unloaded from trains and trucks by cranes at the side of docks. Three quarters of the hull of a fully-loaded container ship is underwater, so it can only sail into deep-water harbors. The biggest container ships are so large that they need an area about 5 mi. (8km) in which to stop and a circle of over 1 mi. (1.6km) to turn in.

What large wooden ships were driven by oars?

Some of the most successful ships built by early civilizations were the galleys of the Phoenicians and Greeks and the longships of the Vikings (right). All of these ships were low and narrow. Usually equipped with a single mast and a square sail, they also came with rows of oars. This design made the ships versatile—they could sail across the sea to another country, be rowed up rivers, and slip into shallow, sheltered harbors. When they went on raids, the Vikings would attach their painted shields to the side of the boat and use the oars for maximum speed. Viking cargo ships were similar to longships in shape, but cargo ships were higher and wider. The largest ones could carry up to 38 tons of cargo.

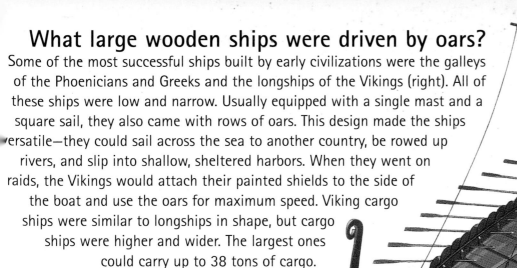

How does a hydrofoil work?

Hydrofoils (left) are ships that seem to fly through the water on underwater "wings" called foils. The foils are attached to the ship using stilts. When the ship is powered forward, the foils produce a lifting force—just like an airplane's wings do in the air. As the boat gathers speed the hull is lifted right out of the water. Because the foils slice through the water with so little drag, hydrofoils can travel at speeds of up to 92 mph (148km/h).

Quick-fire Quiz

1. How much of a loaded container ship is underwater?
a) One half
b) One quarter
c) Three quarters

2. What does a submarine need to do before it can resurface?
a) Fill its tanks up with water
b) Fill its tanks up with air
c) Fire its torpedoes

3. Which kind of ship has wings?
a) A hydrofoil
b) A hovercraft
c) A catamaran

4. How large is a standard container?
a) 33 ft. x 18 ft.
b) 40 ft. x 20 ft.
c) 40 ft. x 8 ft.

Ocean Adventures

For tens of thousands of years people have explored the oceans searching for new lands to settle on and goods to trade. Today ships cross the oceans at previously unimaginable speeds, while underwater craft explore the mysterious world beneath the waves. Yet even with the help of submersibles, we still know less about the bottom of the ocean than we do about the surface of the moon.

How deep can submersibles dive?

Submersibles are small underwater craft built to withstand the crushing pressure deep beneath the ocean. One of the most successful submersibles is the U.S. *Alvin* (right). It has made thousands of dives since it was built in 1964, carrying three people to depths of 14,765 ft. (4,500m). One of *Alvin's* most spectacular discoveries was finding deep-sea vents in the 1970s. But *Alvin* is not the deepest-diving submersible. The U.S. *Sea Cliff*, the Russian *Mir*, the French *Nautile*, and the Japanese *Shinkai* can all dive to 19,685 ft. (6,000m) and are able to explore everywhere except the deepest ocean trenches.

How long can scuba divers stay underwater?

Scuba stands for "Self-Contained Underwater Breathing Apparatus." It was invented in 1943 by the Frenchmen Jacques Cousteau and Emile Gagnan. Scuba divers carry tanks filled with air on their backs (below) and can dive for about an hour. Scuba divers can move freely because they carry their own air supply and do not have to wear bulky, heavy diving suits.

Jacques Cousteau

How did ancient people explore the oceans?

Although we have no information on the earliest seagoing vessels, we know that people sailed from Southeast Asia to Australia and New Guinea at least 40,000 years ago. From around 1500 B.C. Polynesian sailors settled on all the main islands in the middle of the Pacific Ocean within a triangle bounded by Hawaii, New Zealand, and Easter Island. It is believed they used two canoes joined together, with a platform in the middle (left) to carry passengers, animals, and plants across the ocean.

Which was the first ship to cross the Atlantic Ocean on steam power?

Although the first steamship to cross the Atlantic was the *Savannah* in 1819, it sailed most of the way. Not until 1838 did a small, 700-ton paddler, the *Sirius* (left), complete the whole journey on steam power alone. During the last part of the 19-day voyage, however, the *Sirius* ran out of coal and had to burn its cargo! Brunel's *Great Western* began its crossing four days after the *Sirius* but arrived in New York City just a few hours later, thanks to the efforts of the crew, who kept the engines running at full speed night and day.

Who first sailed around the world alone?

The first person to sail around the world alone was Joshua Slocum. He set sail aboard his homemade craft, the *Spray*, in 1898 and completed 45,730 mi. (73,600km) in 1,158 days—stopping several times along the way. In 1969 Robin Knox-Johnson became the first person to sail around the world alone nonstop. He took 312 days and one hour to travel 29,949 mi. (48,197km) in his yacht *Suhaili*.

How are satellites used to explore oceans today?

Nowadays the oceans can be explored without traveling on or under the ocean. High above Earth, satellites in space are studying the oceans—constantly monitoring surface temperatures, the speed and direction of currents, sea levels, wave heights, sea ice, and even levels of plant life. This information helps scientists understand more about how the oceans work and is useful to engineers seeking new offshore gas and oil reserves. Satellites also send signals to ships' computers (right), helping them plot their positions accurately.

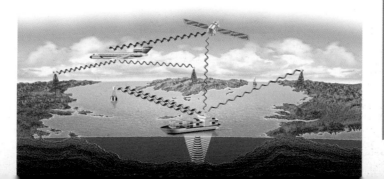

Quick-fire Quiz

1. Which sailors settled on islands in the Pacific from 1500 B.C.?
a) Octanesians
b) Polynesians
c) Tetranesians

2. What is the greatest depth that submersibles can dive to?
a) 14,765 ft.
b) 6,562 ft.
c) 19,685 ft.

3. Who was the first person to sail around the world without stopping?
a) Robin Knox-Johnson
b) Jacques Cousteau
c) Joshua Slocum

4. For how long can scuba divers stay underwater?
a) About 30 minutes
b) About 1 hour
c) About 2 hours

Ocean and River Facts

Oceans dominate Earth's surface. The Pacific Ocean alone covers more area than all of the continents put together. Key facts about some of the world's best-known rivers, lakes, and oceans are recorded here.

Atlantic Ocean
- **Area:** 31.663 million sq. mi. (82 million sq km). Earth's second largest ocean.
- **Average depth:** 10,925 ft. (3,330m).
- **Maximum depth:** 30,000 ft. (9,144m).
- **Volume:** 421.1 billion yd³ (311.93 billion m³).
- **Ocean currents:** Gulf Stream, Labrador Current, North Atlantic Current, Equatorial Current, Canaries Current, Brazil Current.
- **Special features:** Mid-Atlantic Ridge has the world's largest mountain range. Has the most shallow seas: Gulf of Mexico, Caribbean Sea, Mediterranean Sea.

Pacific Ocean
- **Area:** 64.098 million sq. mi. (166 million sq km). Earth's largest ocean.
- **Average depth:** 14,040 ft. (4,280m). Earth's deepest ocean.
- **Maximum depth:** 36,160 ft. (11,022m) in the Challenger Deep, Mariana Trench.
- **Volume:** 977 billion yd³ (724 billion m³).
- **Ocean currents:** North Equatorial Current, North Pacific Current, California Current, Kuroshio Current, Oyashio Current, Alaska Current, South Equatorial Current, West Wind Drift, Peru Current, East Australia Current, Equatorial Countercurrent.
- **Special features:** "Ring of fire" of volcanic activity around its edge. Mid-ocean ridges include the East Pacific Rise, Galapagos Rise, and Chile Rise.

Antarctic Ocean
- **Area:** 13.515 million sq. mi. (35 million sq km).
- **Average depth:** 13,123 ft. (4,000m).
- **Maximum depth:** 23,737 ft. (7,235m).
- **Volume:** 189 billion yd³ (140 billion m³).
- **Ocean currents:** Antarctic Circumpolar Current—carrying 175.5 yd³ (130 million m³) of water per second, ten times the flow of all world's rivers together.
- **Special features:** Sea ice—1.55 million sq. mi. (4 million sq km) are permanently frozen. In the winter a further 8.1 million sq. mi. (21 million sq km) freeze over.

Indian Ocean
- **Area:** 28.42 million sq. mi. (73.6 sq km). Earth's third largest ocean.
- **Average depth:** 12,762 ft. (3,890m).
- **Maximum depth:** 24,442 ft. (7,450m).
- **Volume:** 394.377 billion yd³ (292,131 billion m³).
- **Ocean currents:** South Equatorial Current, West Australia Current, Agulhas Current, North Equatorial Current, Equatorial Countercurrent.
- **Special features:** Y-shaped mid-ocean ridge. Climate dominated by monsoon winds. Many coral islands.

Arctic Ocean
- **Area:** 5.775 million sq. mi. (14.956 million sq km). Smallest ocean.
- **Average depth:** 3,250 ft. (990m). Shallowest ocean.
- **Maximum depth:** 18,051 ft. (5,502m).
- **Volume:** 22.95 billion yd³ (17 billion m³).
- **Ocean currents:** Transarctic Current.
- **Special features:** Four minor basins and three ocean ridges. 10,000–50,000 icebergs drift south each year, taking two percent of the ocean's water. In the winter, sea ice—average thickness 9.8–11.5 ft. (3–3.5m)—covers 5.8 million sq. mi. (15 million sq km) of the Arctic Ocean.

Nile River

- **Length:** 4,160 mi. (6,695km). Longest river in the world.
- **Location:** White Nile flows through Uganda, Sudan, and Egypt. Blue Nile flows through Ethiopia, Zaire, Kenya, Tanzania, Rwanda, and Burundi.
- **Sources:** Lake Victoria (White Nile) and Lake Tana (Blue Nile).
- **Drainage basin:** 1.293 million sq. mi. (3.349 million sq km).
- **Average discharge:** 4,050 yd³ (3,000 m³) per second.
- **Special features:** Aswan Dam holds back one of the world's largest artificial lakes—Lake Nasser.

Amazon River

- **Length:** 4,002 mi. (6,440km). Second longest river in the world.
- **Location:** Brazil.
- **Sources:** Many sources in the Andes mountains.
- **Drainage basin:** Over 2.5 million sq. mi. (7 million sq km).
- **Average discharge:** 243,000 yd³ (180,000 m³) per second. This flow reduces saltiness of the Atlantic Ocean up to 100 mi. (160km) offshore.
- **Special features:** At its mouth the Amazon River is 150 mi. (240km) wide.

Yangtze River

- **Length:** 3,988 mi. (6,418km). Third longest river in the world.
- **Location:** China.
- **Source:** Mount Gelandandong, Tibet.
- **Drainage basin:** 756.429 sq. mi. (1.959 sq km).
- **Average discharge:** 45,900 yd³ (34,000 m³) per second.
- **Special features:** Large ships can reach 684 mi. (1,100km) upriver. Passes through three gorges with walls as high as 3,280 ft. (1,000m).

Lake Victoria

- **Area:** 26,828 sq. mi. (69,480 sq km). Second largest freshwater lake in the world.
- **Depth:** 269 ft. (82m).
- **Volume:** 3.726 million yd³ (2.76 million m³).
- **Coastline:** 2,000 mi. (3,220km).
- **Tributaries:** 22 rivers and streams.
- **Special features:** Has over 200 species of fish.

Lake Superior

- **Area:** Over 31,700 sq. mi. (82,100 sq km). Largest freshwater lake in the world.
- **Depth:** 482 ft. (147m).
- **Volume:** 16.335 million yd³ (12.1 million m³).
- **Coastline:** 2,725 mi. (4,385km).
- **Tributaries:** 20 rivers and streams, including the Nipigon River and St. Louis River.
- **Special features:** One of the five Great Lakes. Second only to Lake Baikal in volume—contains ten percent of the world's freshwater.

Lake Baikal

- **Area:** 12,163 sq. mi. (31,500 sq km).
- **Depth:** 5,370 ft. (1,637m). Deepest lake in the world.
- **Volume:** 31.05 million yd³ (23 million m³).
- **Coastline:** 1,305 mi. (2,100km).
- **Tributaries:** 336 rivers and streams.
- **Special features:** At 25–50 million years old, it is believed to be the world's oldest lake. Contains 20 percent of the world's freshwater. The sediment on the lakebed is estimated to be 4.5 mi. (7km) deep. Provides a habitat for more than 1,200 animal species—three quarters of which are found nowhere else, including the world's only freshwater seal.

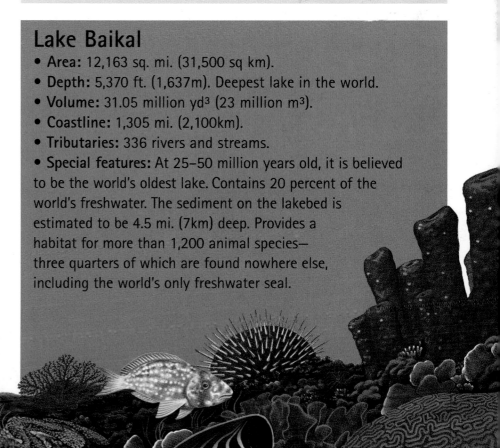

Index

Quick-fire Quiz ANSWERS

Page 5 Water in Our World
1. b   2. b   3. a   4. b

Page 7 World's Oceans
1. b   2. a   3. b   4. b

Page 9 Seas of the World
1. c   2. c   3. c   4. a

Page 11 The Ocean Floor
1. a   2. a   3. b   4. b

Page 13 Islands and Reefs
1. c   2. b   3. b   4. c

Page 15 Ocean Currents
1. b   2. a   3. b   4. c

Page 17 Oceans and Climate
1. b   2. b   3. a   4. a

Page 19 Waves and Tides
1. a   2. a   3. b   4. c

Page 21 Coasts
1. c   2. a   3. b   4. c

Page 23 A River's Journey
1. b   2. c   3. c   4. c

Page 25 River Landscapes
1. b   2. a   3. c   4. c

Page 27 Where Rivers Meet ...
1. c   2. a   3. a   4. c

Page 29 Lakes
1. b   2. b   3. b   4. a

Page 31 Water Under the Ground
1. b   2. a   3. a   4. a

Page 33 People, Oceans, and Rivers
1. a   2. b   3. b   4. b

Page 35 Watercraft
1. c   2. b   3. a   4. c

Page 37 Ocean Adventures
1. b   2. c   3. a   4. b